To Jean Brooker who started the whole idea

A a

apple

Apples are picked in the late summer and autumn, when they are ripe.

Farm
ALPHABET BOOK

Farm ALPHABET BOOK

Jane Miller

M

MACMILLAN CHILDREN'S BOOKS

The author would like to thank the following for their
invaluable help and assistance with this book:
June Armstrong
Richard Baker and Andrew Budd, Preshaw Estate, Hampshire
Patricia Blake
Keira Glen
Sue Latham
Poultry World
Norman Simmons
Yeo Bros. (A. N. Yeo) Ltd., Bristol

First published 1981 by J. M. Dent & Sons Ltd

Picturemac edition published 1990 by
Macmillan Children's Books
A division of Macmillan Publishers Limited
London and Basingstoke
Associated companies throughout the world

Reprinted 1990

ISBN 0–333–51448–3

A CIP catalogue record for this book is available from the British Library

Printed in Hong Kong

Bb

bull

A bull is a calf's father.
It is a large, strong animal.

Cc

calf

A calf is a young cow or young bull.

D d

donkey

Donkeys
graze in
the fields
when they
are not
pulling carts.

E e

egg

Birds lay
eggs.
These eggs
were laid
by a hen.

Ff

foal

A foal is a young horse.
Its mother is a mare.
Its father is a stallion.

G g

goat

A young goat
is a kid.
Its mother is
a nanny-goat.
Its father is
a billy-goat.

H h

hen

A hen is the
mother of
a chick.
The chick's
father is
a cockerel.

I i

incubator

An incubator
keeps eggs
warm.
After 21 days
chicks
hatch out
of the eggs.

Jj

jam

Jam is made from fruit boiled with sugar and water.

K k

kitten

A kitten is
a young cat.

Ll

lamb

A lamb is a young sheep.
Its mother is a ewe.
Its father is a ram.

Mm

mouse

A mouse sleeps during the day and finds its food at night.

N n

nest

Nests are built by birds to lay their eggs in. This is a coot's nest.

O
o

orchard

**Fruit trees
grow in
orchards.**

P p

pig

This is a mother pig, called a sow.
A father pig is a boar.
A young pig is a piglet.

Q q

quill

A quill is a
large feather.
It grows in
a bird's wing
or tail.
A quill can be
used as a pen.

Rr

rabbit

Tame rabbits are kept as pets. Wild rabbits live in burrows under the ground.

S
s

swan

A mother
swan teaches
her cygnets
to swim
as soon
as they are
hatched.

Tt

tractor

Tractors pull machines on the farm.

Uu

umbrella

Umbrellas keep people dry when it rains.

V v

vegetable

Vegetables are grown on farms and in gardens.

W
W

web

Webs are
spun by
spiders.
In these they
catch insects
to eat.

Xx

X

X shows that this sheep
and lamb
belong to the farmer.

Y y

yolk

A yolk is the yellow part of an egg.

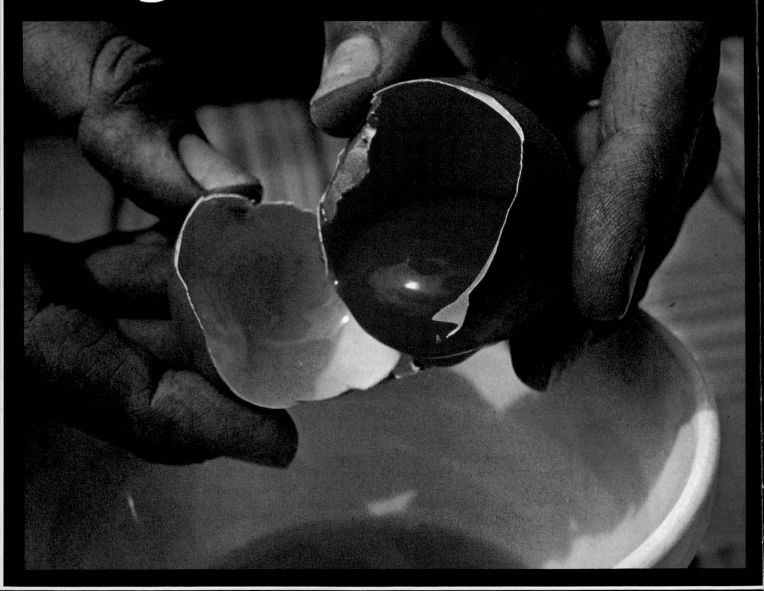

Z z

zip

Zips open and close all kinds of clothes worn on the farm.

Jane Miller was born and brought up in Australia.
At the age of ten she was taking photographs of the animals
she owned, and processing them herself using a printing frame
and printing-out paper. Before coming to London in 1958,
Jane Miller visited Thailand and India where she took many
photographs that have since been published. She subsequently
trained as a free-lance photographer and began to work
professionally, travelling widely in the British Isles.
She died in 1989.